Catalogue of Violent and Destructive Earthquakes in the Philippines

Miguel Saderra Masó

CATALOGUE OF VIOLENT AND DESTRUCTIVE EARTHQUAKES IN THE PHILIPPINES (1599-1909).

Introduction.—The occasion for publishing this catalogue of Philippine earthquakes which were of violent and destructive character has been furnished by a request from Prof. John Milne for a list of such phenomena, to be included in the General Earthquake Catalogue which this eminent seismologist is preparing under the auspices of the British Association for the Advancement of Science. The said general catalogue has been undertaken with a view toward reducing to uniformity and completing those published years ago by Robert Mallet (1859) and Perrey (1844-1871). The form adopted for Professor Milne's new catalogue is very concise, comprising only the date, intensity, and region together with principal localities affected. It will contain only the earthquakes of intensities VII to X according to the scale of De Rossi-Forel, and these will be divided into three classes: Class I will be formed by the earthquakes of sufficient force to produce cracks in buildings and to throw down chimneys; they correspond to force VII of De Rossi-Forel. Class II consists of the earthquakes which not only threw down chimneys but also walls and some weak structures; force VIII of De Rossi-Forel. Class III comprises the earthquakes which caused general destruction; force IX and X of De Rossi-Forel. As this classification is as purely conventional as every other and adopted only in the catalogue mentioned, we do not employ it in the present catalogue of Philippine earthquakes, but retain the almost universally adopted scale of De Rossi-Forel. We shall also present more details as to the towns and buildings damaged, the number of victims and other disastrous effects than enter into the catalogue of Professor Milne.

Hence, the differences between the list prepared for Professor Milne

3

as well as the partial catalogue published in our Monthly Bulletin for February of the present year consist in the following: (1) This catalogue contains also several earthquakes whose intensities were between VI and VII, while in the former only such figure as according to their effects were decidedly of force VII. (2) The new catalogue is more complete as to details concerning the towns, etc., which have been destroyed.

It is to be regretted that we are unable to present here a complete historical catalogue of all the destruction wrought in the Archipelago by earthquakes since the time when Legaspi and Urdaneta first set foot on these shores. But the old chroniclers, who dwell upon the political happenings with an attention to detail which is occasionally overdone, were invariably laconic when there was question of earthquakes and similar natural phenomena; as a rule they were satisfied with mentioning the occurrence in a general and therefore vague way, without any attempt at precision as to dates and places. Still the writers in the Philippines did nothing worse than imitate their colleagues throughout the rest of the world. This fact is responsible for the great contrast exhibited by our catalogue as regards the number and details of earthquakes which occurred prior to 1800, records of which have been preserved, and the same data for the period from 1800 to the present time. This same difference is observable in all catalogues of a similar nature, even in those which cover phenomena which occurred in Europe. As to the Philippine writers, an additional excuse is found in the peculiar conditions of life in these Islands. As far as we know, only two earthquakes which took place during the period which alone can come under consideration—that is, since the discovery of the Archipelago—have claimed a considerable number of victims, and these in the capital, because outside of Manila—if we except two or three of the principal cities—the buildings which could become dangerous during an earthquake have always been few.

Moreover, in a country in which fires consume every year thousands of dwellings and where the terrible typhoons frequently destroy whole towns with heavy loss of lives, the damage done by earthquakes has rarely been so great as to impress those occurrences indelibly upon the memory. This is beyond doubt one of the reasons why prior to the beginning of the nineteenth century hardly any data can be found concerning the numerous earthquakes which during the preceding two centuries must have occurred in the Visayas and above all on the large Island of Mindanao.

The first earthquake of which the chronicles contain a mention is that of 1599. There is no reasonable doubt that during the twenty-eight years which had then elapsed since the founding of Manila by Legaspi, several strong and possibly even destructive earthquakes occurred in this part of Luzon Island, but, as the author of the "Verdadera relación de la grande destrucción * * * del año 1645" tells us, "when first founded, Manila consisted of wooden houses roofed with a certain kind of palm leaves, the same which the natives use in their buildings." Hence the damage done by these earthquakes must have been insignificant. Much more terrible were the losses caused by conflagrations which within a few years twice wiped out the entire city.

The first Bishop of Manila, Domingo de Salazar, seeing the city exposed to such general destructions by fire like the one of February 14, 1583, gave the first impulse to the construction of stone buildings and worked indefatigably in this direction. In person he explored the surroundings of Manila in quest of stone quarries and by the middle of the year 1591 he had nearly finished his palace and the cathedral, when financial difficulties caused a temporary suspension of the work. At the same time a great number of public and private buildings were under construction. The enthusiasm for structures of stone or brick with tile roofs did not diminish during the next fifty years. The chroniclers tell us that "the Spaniards began to build their houses of stone and tiles without the so necessary precautions against earthquakes. * * * Beautiful structures and dwelling houses were reared, so high and spacious that they resembled palaces; magnificent churches with lofty and graceful towers, within the walls of Manila as well as outside of them: all of which made the city very beautiful and gay and contributed equally to health and pleasure." The disaster of 1645, commonly called the earthquake of St. Andrew, as it occurred on the feast of this apostle, November 30, razed nearly every one of these buildings to the ground, and since then the style and appearance of buildings has changed greatly throughout the Archipelago, with a correspondingly great saving of lives in the subsequent earthquakes.

Masonry arches were henceforth banished from the churches; the heavy walls of the latter were further strengthened by massive buttresses; and the towers were given truly enormous substructures. But even with these precautions there is at present hardly one out of the hundreds of churches built during the seventeenth and eighteenth centuries which did not some time or other require important repairs of its masonry work or even partial reconstruction owing to earthquake damages. The only structure of this class which thus far has withstood all convulsions, is the church of St. Agustin, Manila. Nevertheless, as we have stated before, the chroniclers hardly mention all this destruction, except in a very general and cursory manner. I do not hesitate to say: they were accustomed to see similar havoc created nearly every year in one part of the Archipelago or the other by some severe typhoon, accompanied by far greater loss of lives and property, and consequently much more felt by the people than the destruction of a church, *convento*, municipal building ("tribunal"), one or two bridges, or other masonry structure.

In the present catalogue our aim has been to present all that is known of the various violent and destructive earthquakes on record. The first column of each page contains the ordinal number of the disturbance for purposes of reference. In the second, the date is given as accurately as it could be ascertained, Roman numerals being used to designate the months. Unfortunately, of some earthquakes only the year is known; of others, the year and month. Of one (No. 32) the approximate hour has been recorded, but not the day of the month; while of another (No. 38) the hour has been preserved for posterity, but whether the phenomenon occurred during February or March, the records leave undecided. In the third column will be found, in the first place, the intensity of the disturbance, Roman numerals representing the degrees of the scale of De Rossi-Forel (I-X); then the region affected most, and finally the damages caused, if known, and other information, if available.

In describing the epicentral regions, the present distribution of the Archipelago into provinces has been used throughout the catalogue. This division is shown on the first of the two maps of the Philippines which accompany this catalogue (Plate I). As to the designation "Benguet" occasionally occurring in the text where provinces are enumerated, but not found on the map, we beg to offer the excuse that the region thus named is exceedingly well known in the Philippines as it contains Baguio, *the* health resort of the Islands. For the readers outside of the Archipelago we remark that Benguet is at present a subprovince of the Mountain Province, of which it forms the southernmost part. The location of Baguio is shown on the map on Plate II. A similar remark applies to Lepanto and Bontoc, likewise divisions of the Mountain Province, whose capitals, Cervantes and Bontoc, are indicated on the same map.

As we would hardly be justified in assuming that every reader is in possession of a detailed map of the Philippines, and a knowledge of the general distribution and the main directions of the principal mountain systems of an earthquake country is important, we add a second map on which these data are shown by means of dashes, together with the most important seismic regions, and the positions of the principal towns, bays, etc., mentioned in the text. (Plate II.)

Near the left margin of this second map will be found an index of the seismic regions just mentioned, each of them being represented by its ordinal number (large Roman figures). Near each of these ordinals is placed the corresponding number of earthquakes since 1862 contained in the catalogue (Arabic figures), which is followed, in brackets, by an analysis of the said number, in which Roman figures designate the degrees of the earthquake, scale of De Rossi-Forel, while small Arabic figures, written like exponents, give the number of earthquakes of each degree of intensity.

In drawing the map on Plate II it was not intended to represent the epicentric area of every individual earthquake center (which would have crowded the map beyond reasonable limits), but rather to show the principal seismic regions. Hence most of these curves contain more than one focus. The approximate position of each of the latter has, however, been indicated by a star, while the figure placed close to the star gives the number of earthquakes which proceeded from the said center.

A word must be said in apology for the constant use in the following list of the Spanish word "*convento*." This word which means monastery, cloister, or convent, is universally used in the Philippines to designate also the habitation of the clergy attached to a parish church. Although these are, as a rule, spacious buildings and were formerly inhabited well-nigh exclusively by friars, they can not properly be called monasteries. Wherefore, in order to avoid lengthy circumlocutions, the Spanish word "*convento*" has been retained.

7

The reader who is not familiar with this country may find it strange that in reporting earthquake damages so much emphasis appears to be laid on the harm done to churches and *conventos*. This is easily explained by the fact that these buildings were often the only structures within the meizoseismal area, and built nearly everywhere in the most substantial manner.

In the present catalogue we have also included, by way of an appendix, the earthquakes which are known to have occurred in the Marianas or Ladrones group of islands. While their number is too small to warrant separate publication, we believe that the data concerning them will be welcome to the earthquake investigator.

CATALOGUE OF VIOLENT AND DESTRUCTIVE EARTHQUAKES IN THE PHILIPPINES.

No. Date. Intensity. Epicenter and effects. *Y. M. d. h. m.* 1 1599 VI 25 3 20 IX Manila and neighboring provinces. Damaged many private buildings in Manila; cracked the vault of the Jesuit Church so badly that it had to be demolished and replaced by a ceiling; fissured the walls and ruined the roof of Santo Domingo Church. 2 1600 I 2 0 0 VIII Earthquake of destructive force and long duration in Manila; extent of damage unknown. 3 1600 XI — — — VI Violent and protracted earthquake. 4 1601 I 16 0 — VIII Manila and adjacent provinces. Did considerable damage to some churches and many private houses in Manila. Its duration was unusually great, it being said that during 7 minutes the shocks were almost continuous. There were several dead and a great number of injured. The repetitions were frequent throughout the year. 5 1608 XII 3 — — VI-VII Leyte Island. Violent chiefly in the country around Dulag and Palo (E coast of northern Leyte). It does not appear to have been destructive. 6 1610 XI — — — IX Manila and provinces east of it. Several writers call it a "terrible earthquake which progressed from E to W." 7 1620 — — — — IX Panay Island. Great convulsions of the ground; the Aclan River changed its course. The few stone buildings in the affected districts, as, for instance, the church at Passi, Province of Iloilo, were badly cracked, the wooden structures either fell, owing to the snapping of the uprights, or remained inclined in various directions. The provinces which suffered most were those of Iloilo and Capiz. 8 1627 VIII — — — X Northern Luzon. The historians mention it as one of the earthquakes which caused the greatest convulsions in northern Luzon, especially in Ilocos Norte and Cagayan, but above all in the region of the Central Central Cordillera, Lepanto, and Bontoc. The data are somewhat vague. It is said that part of the northern Caraballo Mountains subsided. 9 1628 — — — — IX Camarines and Albay. A destructive earthquake in which, it is said, a mountain burst and emitted a river of water and mud which swept away the town of Camarines and others. The name of

Camarines was at the time used to designate the present town of Camalig and the district near the southern slopes of Mayon Volcano. The flood mentioned was probably an avalanche of water, sand, volcanic ashes, and lapilli, such as also on other occasions have occurred on the slopes of the same volcano during periods of torrential rains. No. Date. Intensity. Epicenter and effects. *Y. M. d. h. m.* 10 1636 XII 21 — — IX Western Mindanao. Destructive earthquake. The epicenter appears to have been in Illana Bay. Great landslides are reported to have occurred at Point Flechas which is between the Bays of Illana and Sibuguey. 11 1641 I 4 — — X Northern Luzon. Destructive earthquake, accompanied by great landslides in the mountains and eruptions of water and mud in the region of northern Luzon which comprises the Provinces of the Ilocos, of Cagayan, and the Cordillera Central. All the historians of the Archipelago mention this cataclysm which occurred shortly after the almost simultaneous eruptions of Sanguir and Jolo. 12 1645 XI 30 20 — X The most terrible earthquake recorded in the annals of the Archipelago. It might almost be said that from Manila to Cagayan and Ilocos Norte it left no stone upon the other. In the capital, where during the preceding fifty years a great number of stone buildings had been erected, magnificent churches, palaces, and public buildings, as well as private residences and villas, the destruction was frightful. Ten churches were wrecked entirely, to wit: the Royal Chapel, Cathedral, Santo Domingo, those of the Recollects and Franciscans, Santiago, San Antonio, Nuestra Señora de Guia, and the parish churches of Binondo and San Miguel; only San Agustin and the Jesuit Church remained standing. Twelve monasteries, colleges, and hospitals were likewise converted into ruins. No better fared the palace of the Governor-General, the Real Audiencia and up to 150 of the finest residences which, as one author puts it, "in other cities would have been considerable palaces." The rest of the private houses were damaged to so great an extent that the majority had to be demolished. The number of persons killed exceeded 600 and the total of killed and injured is stated to have been 3,000.

Outside of Manila there was a general destruction of villas and other buildings which had been erected on both banks of the Pasig River. Throughout the neighboring provinces the masonry structures built by the missionaries suffered the same fate as those in Manila. From the farthest provinces in the north were reported great alterations of the surface with

10

almost complete disappearance of some native villages, changes in the courses of rivers, subsidences of plains, eruptions of sand, etc. All the writers of the time qualify this disturbance as the most disastrous earthquake not only in Luzon, but likewise in Mindoro, Marinduque, and the other islands south of Luzon. On the other hand, the provinces of Camarines and Albay appear to have suffered little or nothing. 13 1645 XII 5 23 — VIII The earthquake of November 30 was followed by almost daily repetitions and countless aftershocks, one of which, on December 5, was of such intensity as to finish the wrecking of many buildings, "leaving [as a chronicler writes] the city in such condition that it was impossible to walk through it." Aftershocks of variable force continued to be very frequent throughout an entire year; that is, until the end of 1646. No. Date. Intensity. Epicenter and effects. *Y. M. d. h. m.* 14 1646 III — — — VI According to several chroniclers, the aforementioned aftershocks were more were more frequent and of greater intensity during the month of March, some of them assuming a violent character. 15 1648 — — — — VIII Southern Luzon. Very violent earthquake, damaging many buildings (Von Hoff). 16 1653 V 1 — — VI Earthquake in Manila and surrounding provinces. 17 1658 VIII 20 17 — IX Destructive earthquake. Some historians maintain that it was as severe as that of 1645; but it caused fewer ruins, partly on account of its short duration, partly because it found buildings of less height and greater power or resistance than those erected before 1645. Nevertheless it destroyed the monastery of Santa Clara and did great damage to the churches and monasteries of the Dominicans and Recollects, likewise to the archiepiscopal palace, the Jesuit College, and a considerable number of private buildings. The epicentral region appears to have included only the southern part of Luzon. 18 1665 VI 19 — — VIII Destructive in Manila and adjacent provinces. In the ruins of numerous houses 19 persons perished and many more were injured. Of public buildings only the Jesuit Church is mentioned as having suffered to some extent. 19 1675 II — — — VIII Destructive in northern Mindoro and Batangas Province. Mention is made of extensive landslides, the opening of many fissures and the subsidence of large tracts on the beach of the northeast coast of Mindoro. The repetitions were many and severe. 20 1683 VIII 24 — — VII Damaged some buildings in Manila. 21 1687 II — — — VI Several violent earthquakes, which, however, caused no notable damages. 22 1699 — — — — VII Many chroniclers assure us that during this year and the following destructive earthquakes visited Manila; but there is great confusion as to the days and months in which they occurred. 23 1716 IX 24 — — VII Vicinity of Taal Volcano. Violent in Manila and the Provinces of Rizal, Laguna, Cavite, and Batangas. Connected with an eruption of the volcano. At each spasm of the latter the earth shook so violently that many buildings in Manila and the provinces mentioned suffered much harm, especially those in the vicinity of Lake Bombon, within which is situated the said volcano. 24 1728 XI 28 — — IX Remarkable on account of its having been very perceptible throughout the entire Archipelago. Caused considerable damage in Manila and towns in southern Luzon. 25 1730 — — — — IX Destructive in the Provinces of Tayabas and Laguna; ruined the church and the church and *convento* at Mauban and other buildings in this and other towns of the two provinces. 26 1743 — — — — IX Destructive in Tayabas Province, wrecking masonry structures in the town of Tayabas and others. No. Date. Intensity. Epicenter and effects. *Y. M. d. h. m.* 27 1749 VIII 12 9 — IX A violent eruption of Taal Volcano, which caused great havoc in all the towns on the shores of Lake Bombon. The shocks which accompanied each of the intermittent outbursts of the volcano were so severe that they left hardly any building undamaged throughout the provinces in the neighborhood of Manila—Rizal, Laguna, Cavite, Batangas, Tayabas, and in northern Mindoro. The convulsions of the ground were very remarkable; displacement occurred and fissures, both wide and deep, opened in the entire Province of Batangas and likewise in Cavite Province, up to Lake Bay. As the shocks occurred during many days, the majority of Manila's inhabitants abandoned the Walled City and lived under tents or in structures of bamboo and nipa. The greatest force of the earthquakes and, consequently, the greatest upheavals seem to have occurred in the region stretching from Taal Volcano toward Talim Island (Lake Bay) and the Antipolo Mountain Range.

Repetitions and aftershocks were frequent during nearly a year. 28 1754 V 15 21 — X Another eruption of Taal Volcano, the most terrible in the history of the Islands. All the towns which surrounded Lake Bombon were destroyed completely. When rebuilt, they were placed at a distance from the lake. There occurred most violent earthquakes which produced disasters in the neighboring provinces equal too, if not exceeding those of 1749. The spasms, separated by intervals of greater or less duration, lasted 7 months, the principal outbursts being always accompanied by very intense earthquakes which made themselves felt throughout a large part of Luzon, on Mindoro Island, and northern Panay. 29 1766 XII 7 10 45 VII A violent earthquake, but did very slight damage in Manila. During the month many more earthquakes of less intensity were felt; in fact they had been frequent ever since the preceding August. There exist no data concerning the provinces around Manila. 30 1767 II 8 1 5 VII Manila and neighboring provinces. Violent earthquake, preceded and followed by numerous shocks of smaller intensity. 31 1767 XI 13 15 25 VII Very violent. In Manila a few walls fell and tile roofs sagged. Slight repetitions marked the succeeding days. Nothing is known of the happenings in the near-by provinces. 32 1770 XII — 23 — VIII Destructive earthquake. Mr. Sonnerat states that it wrecked many houses in Manila. This traveler was at the time on board a ship in the very Bay of Manila; hence it is very strange that he does not give the day of the month on which the disaster took place. 33 1771 II 1 — — VIII Very severe earthquake which laid in ruins several buildings in Manila, express mention being made of the Church of Nuestra Señora de Guia in Ermita, a suburb of Manila. This is probably the same disturbance which, according to some writers, in the beginning of February damaged the church of Antipolo and others in La Laguna and Cavite Provinces. 34 1783 IV 19 — — VI Violent earthquake in Dapitan and the whole of northwestern Mindanao. 35 1787 V 13 6 — VIII Very violent in southern Panay, especially in the Province of Iloilo. No. Date. Intensity. Epicenter and effects. *Y. M. d. h. m.* 36 1787 VII 13 7 — X Panay Island. A terrible earthquake which left the whole island strewn with ruins. Of 15 to 20 churches and *conventos* in Iloilo Province only two or three remained standing; in the two other provinces, Capiz and Antique, the destruction was less universal. Even the thick walls of the fort at Iloilo were breached in many places. There were subsidences in the plains and landslides in the mountains and mighty fissures opened. It is stated that the victims were numerous: in one building 15 persons perished. 37 1796 — — — — IX Many writers assert that during this year a most violent earthquake shook Manila and was followed by severe repetitions during the succeeding 20 days. But, although all agree that the quake was destructive,

13

not one of them gives precise information as to its effects. 38 1797 II-III — 14 — VII A violent earthquake but not destructive in Manila took place between February 11 and March 7. It fissured walls and ruined tile roofs. 39 1811 X 5 — — IX Destructive earthquake in Camarines Province. It wrecked many churches, *conventos*, and other buildings throughout the province, from San Miguel Bay to the vicinity of Albay. 40 1814 II 2 — — VII Albay. Violent earthquakes which preceded and accompanied the great eruption of Mayon Volcano, Province of Albay. Several towns situated on the slopes of the mountain were destroyed by this outburst, while others, at a greater distance, suffered less severely. 41 1818 — — — — VII Dapitan, northwestern Mindanao. Several violent earthquakes with countless repetitions distributed through 6 months. 42 1824 I — — — VII Earthquake, violent in Manila and destructive in Cagayan and Isabela Provinces, northeastern Luzon. 43 1824 IX 29 — — IX Central Luzon. Destructive, making many ruins throughout the Provinces of Tayabas, Laguna, Rizal, and Nueva Ecija. The churches of Cavinti and Lukban were destroyed, that of Antipolo and others badly damaged. 44 1824 X 26 — — IX Destructive in Manila and neighboring provinces. Spoiled the Bridge of Spain and the barracks in its vicinity, the church of Saint Francis and others and many private houses. Frightened by the continual repetitions, people left the city to live in nipa houses and under tents. The undulations seemed to come from north-northwest. 45 1828 XI 9 18 30 VIII Destructive earthquake. Damaged several churches in Manila, likewise the prison and many private residences. The shocks appeared to advance from south to north. 46 1830 I 18 17 — IX Southern Luzon. Destructive in the Provinces of Rizal, Laguna, and Tayabas. In Manila the damage was confined to the cracking of walls and the falling of such as had little power of resistance; but toward Laguna and Tayabas the destruction was greater; the complete destruction of the church and *convento* of Mauban is expressly mentioned. No. Date. Intensity. Epicenter and effects. *Y. M. d. h. m.* 47 1836 I 5 — — VII Very violent earthquake in western Mindanao. The epicenter was in Illana Bay. Severe shocks were felt in Cotabato and Zamboanga, 250 kilometers distant from each other. 48 1840 — — — — IX Destructive earthquake in Sorsogon and Masbate. Ruined the masonry buildings. In Sorsogon Bay extensive subsidences occurred; the sea invaded the town, causing great destruction and claiming many victims. 49 1852 IX 16 18 45 IX Central Luzon. Destructive earthquake which made itself felt with violence in the Provinces of Rizal, Laguna, Cavite, Batangas, Tayabas, Bataan, Zambales, Pampanga, Bulacan, and Nueva Ecija. In Manila it damaged severely a great number of buildings, among them the cathedral and the churches of the Jesuits, San Miguel, and Paco, the church and *convento* at Pandacan (near Manila), and many houses. It is stated that the damage was (relatively) vastly greater in the Provinces of Bataan, Cavite, and Batangas, where many fissures opened and subsidences and landslides occurred. The zone most severely chastised seems to have stretched from the Zambales Mountain Range as far as the coasts of Batangas and Northern Mindoro. Aftershocks were frequent until the middle of October. 50 1852 IX 25 — — VI Very strong earthquake in Camarines and Albay Provinces. 51 1852 XII 24 — — IX Destructive earthquake in Batangas Province and northern Mindoro. Ruined many buildings, among which were the church of Taal and the church and *convento* of Bauang; the church of Batangas likewise suffered severely. 52 1853 — — — — VIII Destructive earthquake in Camarines Province. Made ruins in many towns of the southeastern part of the province, express mention being made of the church, *convento*, tribunal, and the schools of Pulangui. 53 1855 III 22 — — VIII Very violent earthquake in southeastern Luzon. Caused likewise some ruins in the Provinces of Camarines, Albay, and Sorsogon. 54 1858 — — — — VI Very strong earthquakes throughout the district of Cotabato and the south of Lanao district; but it is not known whether they caused extensive damages. 55 1862 III 4 17 30 VII Violent earthquake; cracked some buildings in Manila and the neighboring provinces. 56 1862 VII 13 16 2 VII Violent earthquake which displayed its greatest intensity to the east-northeast of Manila, in the vicinity of Casiguran and Baler Bays. Damaged the church and *convento* of Baler. Several aftershocks followed during the next 4 days. 57 1862 IX 9 3 — VIII Ilocos Norte and Cagayan. The epicenter lay within the Central Cordillera. Did some damage to the church of Piddig and to other towns situated near the Cordillera. 58 1862 X 30 12 30 VI Laguna Province. Very strong earthquake, doing slight damage in the towns south of Lake Bay and close to the volcanic cone of Mount Maquiling. No. Date. Intensity. Epicenter and effects. *Y. M. d. h. m.* 59 1863 VI 3 19 20 X Manila and adjacent provinces. A disastrous earthquake, comparable with that of 1645. Laid in ruins the cathedral and nearly all the other churches, except San Agustin, the palace of the Governor-General, the Audiencia, the barracks, warehouses, etc.; all in all, 46 public buildings in ruins and 25 others badly damaged. Of private houses 570 were destroyed, 531 left tottering. Total, 1,172 buildings in ruins or badly damaged. The number of victims was appalling. It is estimated that in Manila and the surrounding towns alone the number of killed reached 400, that of the injured 2,000. The catastrophe likewise involved many towns in Rizal, Laguna, and Cavite, where it destroyed churches and a great number of houses. 60 1863 VI 9 — — VII Violent earthquake which in Manila and neighboring towns brought to the ground several buildings left in a tottering condition by the preceding disturbance. 61 1864 I 3 — — VI Origin, south of Illana Bay. It was felt very strongly both at Zamboanga and Cotabato; the former west, the latter east of the bay mentioned. 62 1865 XI 23 4 — VI Strong earthquake which caused great excitement in Manila and adjacent provinces. 63 1866 XII 29 3 — VII Ilocos Norte. Very violent earthquake. Damaged several buildings at Laoag and in other towns of the province. 64 1867 I 5 9 45 VI Albay Province. Very strong earthquake. 65 1867 III 26 13 — VI Ilocos Norte. Very strong earthquake. Shocks of varying intensity were frequent in this province during the months December, 1866, to April, 1867. 66 1867 XII 27 9 11 VI Samar Island. Very strong and prolonged earthquake. 67 1868 IV 4 — — VI Leyte Island. Very strong earthquake. 68 1868 VI 29 8 11 VI Panay Island. Very strong earthquake in Iloilo and other towns of the southern part of the island. Frequent, but weak shocks had been felt since June 7. 69 1869 VIII 16 15 — IX Masbate Island. Disastrous earthquake. Destroyed the few masonry buildings extant on the island and ruined or inclined hundreds of houses of wood or light materials; large trees fell, fissures opened, and vast landslides occurred in the mountains and along the coasts, especially in the south of the island. Countless repetitions followed, over 100 of the more severe ones having been counted during the first fortnight after the earthquake. 70 1869 X 1 11 35 VIII Neighboring provinces east and south of Manila, and northern Mindoro. On Luzon the provinces chiefly affected were Rizal, Laguna, Cavite, and Batangas. In Manila this earthquake did considerable damage to quite a number of buildings. In the Provinces of Cavite and Batangas a few churches and

16

conventos were wrecked. There was no loss of life. Repetitions were frequent during the 5 days immediately following the earthquake. No. Date. Intensity. Epicenter and effects. *Y. M. d. h. m.* 71 1869 X 23 16 30 VII Very violent earthquake in southern Luzon, especially in Laguna Province. Slightly damaged some buildings. 72 1870 III 2 3 — VI Northeastern Samar. Very strong earthquake. 73 1870 V 23 23 55 VII Northern Luzon. Very violent earthquake in the Provinces of Ilocos Norte, Cagayan, Isabela, and the northern part of the Mountain Province. 74 1870 XI 4 4 — VII Central Mindanao. A violent earthquake whose epicenter lay between the Gulf of Davao and the Province of Misamis. During the months of November and December occurred many repetitions, some of them very intense. 75 1871 II 21 4 — IX Camiguin Island. Destructive earthquake which affected only the extreme north of the island, where subsequently, on the 30th of April, a volcano which had been believed extinct, burst forth again near its base. This great earthquake was the first of a series of shocks which preceded the eruption. It ruined many buildings constructed of wood, and rent asunder the massive walls of the churches at Mambajao and Catarman, while in the mountains it caused many landslides. Between February 21 and April 30, the date of the volcanic eruption, four violent earthquakes were felt on Camiguin and the neighboring Islands of Mindanao, Cebu, Bohol, etc., aside from countless shocks of less intensity. With the eruption, the earthquakes ceased completely. 76 1871 VI 28 5 30 VI District of Davao, southeastern Mindanao. Violent earthquake throughout the region surrounding Davao Gulf, with frequent aftershocks during the ensuing 8 days. 77 1871 VII 11 21 19 VI Very strong earthquake, remarkable for its wide extension, as it was felt strongly in all the provinces of Luzon north of the sixteenth parallel of north latitude. Repetitions were frequent for three or four days. 78 1871 X 4 20 30 VII District of Davao, southeastern Mindanao. A very violent earthquake, shaking the region around the Gulf of Davao. 79 1871 XI 5 9 — VII Surigao, northeastern Mindanao. Very violent and prolonged earthquake in the Province of Surigao; also remarkable for its extension, being felt intensely throughout eastern Mindanao and perceptible on all the Visayan Islands. 80 1871 XI 29 16 30 VII Very violent earthquake in western Mindanao and on the Islands of Basilan and Jolo. It caused slight damage to several buildings at Zamboanga. 81 1871 XII 8 17 30 IX Destructive earthquake throughout the districts of Lanao, Cotabato, and Davao, Mindanao. It is reported that at Cotabato and Pollok not a single building remained standing; the happenings in the Moro villages and forts are not known. Even in Davao, at a distance of 200 kilometers, it developed great violence. Within one hour three series of most violent shocks were experienced, accompanied by subterraneous rumblings. No. Date. Intensity. Epicenter and effects. *Y. M. d. h. m.* 82 1871 XII 9 7 30 VIII Most violent earthquake in the same regions of Lanao and Cotabato, which completed the devastation of the preceding. Also in this earthquake several separate groups of shocks could be distinguished, which occurred within the space of a little more than half an hour. The subterranean noises were much stronger than on the preceding day and caused consternation. During the first few days following these quakes occurred uncounted repetitions, some of which, like the principal earthquakes, were perceptible not only throughout Mindanao, but likewise in the Visayas up to distances exceeding 500 kilometers. 83 1871 XII 19 22 30 VII Very violent earthquake throughout the length of eastern Mindanao, from Surigao to Davao. It was likewise very perceptible on Samar and Leyte Islands. For a number of days there were many repetitions, some of them very intense, notably those which took place on the 21st and 22d. 84 1872 I 26 19 30 VII Violent earthquake close to the coast of Zambales, near the town of Agno. The shock was repeated ten to twelve times, accompanied by subterraneous noises; an extraordinary wave was seen in the sea close to the coast and in the Agno River which empties into the sea near the town. The affected area was very small, which makes it appear probable that the cause must be sought in some displacements in the scarps of the coast. 85 1872 I 27 16 30 VI Very strong earthquake in the Province of Ilocos Norte, followed by numerous repetitions of considerable intensity during the 28th, 29th, and 30th. 86 1872 VII 22 22 50 VI Camarines and Albay. Very strong earthquake, followed by frequent repetitions during the next two days. 87 1872 VIII 24 21 — VI District of Davao, southeastern Mindanao. Very strong and prolonged earthquake in the vicinity of Mount Apo; repetitions somewhat frequent during several days. 88 1872 IX 6 0 — VI Violent earthquake in northern Samar, Catanduanes Island, and the Provinces of Sorsogon and Albay, having its origin to the northeast of San Bernardino Strait. On the same and the following day occurred four repetitions of moderate intensity. 89 1872 IX 10

18

20 20 VI Very strong earthquake in the northern part of the Mountain Province, Luzon, which, during the month, was preceded and followed by other shocks of less intensity. 90 1872 XII 29 11 48 VIII Most violent earthquake in the region southwest of Manila, which is comprised between the Zambales Mountain Range and the northern part of Mindoro. It did considerable damage to buildings in the Provinces of Bataan, Cavite, and Batangas. The towns which suffered most severely were Balanga, Tuy, Nasugbu, Calaca, Balayan, Taal, and Batangas. Several shocks of small intensity preceded the principal quake between 6 and 9 o'clock. 91 1873 I 16 23 45 VI An earthquake which was very strong in Batangas Province and strong in northern Mindoro and the Provinces of Tayabas, Cavite, Laguna, Rizal, and Bulacan. During the preceding days several light shocks had been felt. No. Date. Intensity. Epicenter and effects. *Y. M. d. h. m.* 92 1873 III 18 13 — VIII Southern Samar. Destructive earthquake whose meizoseismic area included only the town of Mercedes—where some walls were thrown down and others cracked—and a few unimportant villages in the vicinity, situated on the Pacific coast, near which was the seat of disturbance. 93 1873 III 31 1 58 VII Northern Luzon. This earthquake was violent in Ilocos Norte, Ilocos Sur, and the Mountain Province. It was remarkable for its duration of nearly one minute. The resulting damage was negligible. 94 1873 VI 11 23 15 VI This earthquake was violent in northeastern Mindoro and very strong on Romblon and Marinduque Islands, likewise in the Province of Batangas. During June, July, and August the same region experienced several shocks of less intensity. 95 1873 XI 14 17 30 VIII Destructive earthquake in Tayabas Province and on Marinduque Island. It caused great harm in towns of Mauban, Lucban, and others in northeastern Tayabas, and likewise at Boac and Santa Cruz on Marinduque. Many repetitions of smaller intensity occurred during that day and the following. 96 1874 I 17 4 — VI Sorsogon Province and Masbate Island. Intense earthquake, followed by frequent light repetitions and five strong earthquakes during the months of February and March. 97 1874 IV 14 6 45 VI Northern Luzon. A very strong earthquake throughout northern Luzon; that is, in the provinces north of the 16th parallel of latitude. Its center appears to have been near the Ilocos coast. 98 1874 VII 8 10 32 VI Central Luzon. Strong earthquake in the Provinces of Pangasinan, Union, Benguet, Nueva Vizcaya,

Isabela, Tarlac, Zambales, Pampanga, Nueva Ecija, and Bulacan. The epicenter was near the shores of Casiguran Bay. 99 1874 VIII 25 6 30 VIII Destructive earthquake in Zamboanga, western Mindanao. It did considerable damage to masonry buildings and overturned walls. Many large fissures opened near the beach of the sea. 100 1874 IX 16 10 9 VII Violent earthquake in central and eastern Luzon, with innumerable repetitions until the end of October. The center lay near Casiguran Bay. The provinces affected most were northern Camarines, Tayabas, Laguna, Rizal, Bulacan, Nueva Ecija, Nueva Vizcaya, and Isabela. 101 1875 III 9 3 30 VII Very violent earthquake in Abra and the Mountain Province. Destroyed some houses and caused landslides on the mountain sides, ruining rice terraces. It was preceded by feeble shocks and followed by many repetitions until the 14th. 102 1876 V 19 11 30 VIII An earthquake which displayed destructive force in the Camarines. Considerable damage resulted to many buildings in Daet, Nueva Caceres, Iriga, Buhi, and some other towns. The duration of this earthquake was quite unusual. Many repetitions were felt during the following five days. 103 1877 VI 2 11 6 VI Very strong earthquake throughout central Luzon. The meizoseismal area comprised the northern and east-northeastern part of Pangasinan Province. The shocks had still considerable force on the southern and northern coast of Luzon, at distances of about 300 kilometers. No. Date. Intensity. Epicenter and effects. *Y. M. d. h. m.* 104 1877 VI 24 7 — VII Very violent earthquake in Batangas and Cavite Provinces, in the vicinity of Taal Volcano. During the 5 hours immediately preceding the quake, seven series of violent shocks were felt. The earthquake cracked many walls in the towns closest to Lake Bombon. 105 1877 VII 5 12 7 VII Violent earthquake in Camarines, which did no damage, but is remarkable on account of its having been felt with considerable force throughout a great part of Luzon and the Visayas. It was followed by very many aftershocks of variable intensity, 20 having been recorded during the first 24 hours following the earthquake. 106 1877 VII 23 16 24 VII Leyte Island. Very violent earthquake, doing some harm in the northern part of the island. 107 1878 VIII 13 12 14 VI Very strong earthquake of great extension. Its epicenter was southwest of Luzon, near the western coast of Cavite and Zambales Provinces. It was felt intensely from Mindoro to the Provinces of Union and Isabela. 108 1878 IX 17 0 50 VII Violent earthquake to the west of the Gulf of Davao, in the neighborhood of Apo Volcano. Many buildings of Davao suffered seriously. Repetitions were frequent until the 22d. 109 1879 VII 1 2 38 X Surigao Peninsula. Destructive earthquake, with disastrous results to buildings and the topography of the region. Not a single stone building remained inhabitable, although some of them, like the church, government house, and prison at Surigao, were of most solid construction. Besides the opening of innumerable fissures and vast landslides on the coasts and in the mountains, there occurred extensive subsidences: several accurate observations seem to prove that a great part of the peninsula was depressed by about 2 feet. In short, this earthquake was one of those which produced the greatest changes of topography experienced in the Philippines. There followed other very strong quakes on July 5, 24, and 28, and August 8, with countless repetitions of less importance during several months. From July 1 to 15 occurred on the average 5 perceptible shocks per day. 110 1879 VIII 29 6 — VI District of Cotabato, Mindanao. Very strong earthquake which closed a series of quakes which had begun on the 10th of the month. Of these, two felt on the 13th and one on the 21st had been rather intense. 111 1879 IX 28 — — VI District of Davao, Mindanao. Very strong earthquake followed by some repetitions. On the 16th of the same month a somewhat less intense earthquake had been felt in the same region. 112 1879 X 14 9 — VII Ilocos Norte. Very violent earthquake which damaged buildings in the town of Baccarra. 113 1879 XII 19 — — VII Ilocos Norte. Very violent earthquake resulting in damaged buildings at Laoag and other towns of the province. 114 1880 III 28 5 4 VI Very strong earthquake in eastern Panay and the northwestern part of Negros Island. 115 1880 VII 15 0 53 VIII Eastern part of Luzon. Destructive earthquake in the Provinces of Tayabas and Laguna. It damaged to some extent all masonry structures, both public and private, in the towns east of Lake Bay. No. Date. Intensity. Epicenter and effects. *Y. M. d. h. m.*   116 1880 VII 18 12 40 IX Central and southern Luzon. Destructive earthquake affecting the Provinces of Tayabas, Cavite, Laguna, Rizal, Bulacan, Bataan, Pampanga, Tarlac, Nueva Ecija, and Pangasinan. In Manila, as well as in the towns of the provinces mentioned, the earthquake did incalculable harm to buildings, besides causing subsidences, fissures, lateral displacements and similar effects, especially in the alluvial lands along the banks of the Rivers Pasig, the Great and Little Pampanga, and the Agno.

21

117 1880 VII 20 15 40 VIII Earthquake of destructive violence in the towns surrounding Lake Bay, especially in those south and west of the lake.

Within the epicentral region of the three preceding earthquakes, which measures about 300 kilometers from north to south and 200 kilometers from east to west, severe damage was done to the principal stone buildings, such as churches, *conventos*, court-houses, schools, and a few private houses, of 112 of the city principal towns. In the of Manila some 30 public buildings (administration buildings, barracks, churches, monasteries, and colleges) and about 200 private houses of strong materials were either wrecked or badly damaged. Fortunately the number of victims was not in proportion to the magnitude of the disaster, neither in Manila nor in the provinces. From the various reports published at the time we conclude that the number of killed did not exceed 20, nor that of the injured 50. 118 1880 IX 23 22 30 VI Strong earthquake along the Zambales coast, western Luzon. Frequent repetitions until October 2d. 119 1881 VII 11 12 35 VI Very strong earthquake in southern Panay and northwestern Negros. 120 1881 VII 27 16 30 VII Violent earthquake in the Province of Nueva Vizcaya. This was the first violent forerunner of the innumerable shocks which during the months of August, September, and October were to spread devastation and terror throughout this province. 121 1881 IX 1 12 20 IX Destructive earthquake in Nueva Vizcaya. 122 1881 IX 18 4 55 VIII Destructive earthquake in Nueva Vizcaya. 123 1881 IX 18 22 40 VIII Destructive earthquake in Nueva Vizcaya. 124 1881 IX 20 14 25 VIII Destructive earthquake in Nueva Vizcaya.

This memorable seismic period of Nueva Vizcaya ended after October 15. During August and September a missionary made a list comprising over 150 distinct earthquakes, without including countless repetitions of smaller intensity. The effects of these earthquakes were more notable by the alterations in the topography of the region than by the damage done to buildings, as the latter were of wood and thatched with cogon grass. The inhabitants were terror-stricken and the authorities had to work hard to prevent a general exodus from the country. 125 1882 IV 10 19 30 VI District of Cotabato, Mindanao. Violent earthquake, preceded by subterraneous rumblings and followed by frequent repetitions. Already during March some very strong shocks had preceded. 126 1882 X 10 16 57 VII Violent earthquake in Camarines Province with several repetitions. No. Date.

Intensity. Epicenter and effects. *Y. M. d. h. m.*   127 1882 XII 6 — — VII Very violent earthquake in the north of Cebu Island and southern Masbate. 128 1883 II 10 3 28 VII Very violent earthquake in Nueva Vizcaya and Benguet Provinces. It had been preceded by a strong shock at 12h 20m of the 6th. 129 1884 I 10 7 22 VII Very violent earthquake near the southern coasts of Camarines Province, followed by a strong quake on the 11th and by numerous repetitions. 130 1884 VI 5 — — VI Very strong earthquake in the Province of Misamis, northern Mindanao. Repeated with the same intensity at 8h and 13h. 131 1884 X 29 4 10 VI Very strong earthquake in the whole south and southeast of Luzon, chiefly in the Provinces of Laguna, Tayabas, Camarines, Albay, and Sorsogon; likewise on Masbate Island. Many repetitions occurred until the end of November. 132 1884 XII 24 5 — VI Samar, Leyte, and northeast Mindanao. Very strong earthquake, with very severe repetitions on the 26th, 27th, and 28th. 133 1885 II 22 15 30 VIII East coast of Mindanao. Destructive earthquake, which did extensive damage to the churches and other buildings of stone or wood and caused mighty fissures and landslides in the mountains as well as in the scarps of the Pacific coast. 134 1885 VII 23 22 45 IX Northwestern Mindanao. Destructive earthquake which ruined several buildings in the towns and villages of the Dapitan district. The origin lay in the east-northeastern part of the Sulu Sea. The disturbance was felt strongly in nearly all of the Visayan Islands, in western Mindanao and the Sulu Archipelago. Repetitions were frequent until the end of October, those of July 31, September 9, September 23, and October 25 being very intense. 135 1885 IX 30 6 — VI Northeastern Mindanao and southeastern Leyte. Very strong earthquake, followed by many repetitions. 136 1885 XI 19 21 31 VII Very violent earthquake in the Provinces of Nueva Vizcaya, Isabela, and Benguet, followed by strong repetitions on December 8, 19, and 27. 137 1886 IV 10 8 — VI Very strong earthquake in the southeast of Panay and northwest of Negros Islands. 138 1887 II 2 23 — IX Panay Island. Destructive earthquake, causing notable damages, especially in the towns of the Provinces of Iloilo and Capiz. The two days following the earthquake brought many aftershocks. 139 1887 III 24 21 14 VIII Camarines Province. Destructive earthquake doing considerable harm in several towns in the vicinity of Nueva Caceres. The 25th witnessed a very intense repetition, while lighter aftershocks were frequent until the month of May. 140 1888 I 27 3 45 VI Very strong earthquake in eastern Mindanao, which had its epicenter in the Agusan River Valley. 141 1888 VIII 19 14 39 VI Northeastern Luzon. Very strong earthquake, especially in the Provinces of Cagayan and Isabela, followed by many repetitions of varying intensity. No. Date. Intensity. Epicenter and effects. *Y. M. d. h. m.* 142 1889 I 1 10 20 VII Northeastern Mindanao. Violent earthquake in the districts of Surigao and Butuan. Repeated with equal force at 21h 40m of the 12th, doing slight damage to buildings in Surigao, Placer, and Gigaquit, and opening numerous fissures in the ground. Repetitions were very frequent throughout the month, more than 100 having been recorded until the 22d. 143 1889 II 5 15 53 VIII Western Mindanao. Destructive earthquake whose origin lay south of Illana Bay. It was felt with equal force at Zamboanga and Cotabato, each at a distance of more than 100 kilometers from the epicenter, but did no harm worth mentioning. 144 1889 V 26 2 23 VIII Destructive earthquake in the Province of Batangas and northern Mindoro. It wrecked the church at Ibaan and severely damaged the church and other buildings in Batangas, Bauang, Calapan, and several other towns. 145 1889 X 6 11 10 VII Very violent earthquake throughout eastern Mindanao, with epicenter in the valley of the Agusan River. It was very perceptible in every part of the island and on many of the Visayas. 146 1890 II 7 0 10 VIII Destructive earthquake in northern Leyte which split walls in Barugo, Carigara, and other towns, and produced large fissures in the lowlands along the coast. On the 7th and 8th occurred 2 strong and more than 20 light repetitions. 147 1890 IV 13 14 4 VI Northern Luzon. Very strong earthquake in Ilocos Norte and Sur, the Mountain Province, Cagayan, and Isabela. A repetition occurring at 20h developed the same intensity. 148 1891 VI 25 20 10 VII Very violent earthquake in eastern Mindanao whose center was in the Agusan River Valley. Slightly damaged buildings at Davao and Butuan, situated 100 kilometers south and north, respectively, of the focus. 149 1892 III 8 — — VIII Batanes Islands. Destructive earthquake. All that is known of the effects is that it wrecked some buildings at Santo Domingo and other towns on Batan Island. 150 1892 III 16 20 58 X Disastrous earthquake in the Provinces of Pangasinan, Union, and Benguet. It created great havoc in the masonry buildings, such as churches, *conventos*, court-houses, and schools, besides a few private houses, of 30 of the principal towns within the meizoseismic area, produced great fissures and extensive subsidences in the alluvial plains, and many landslides in the steep mountains of northern Pangasinan. Luckily the falling buildings killed only one or two persons. Repetitions were frequent up to the end of the month; of these three occurring on the 17th and one each on the 26th and 28th were of exceptional intensity. 151 1892 III 17 0 34 VII Very violent earthquake in the region mentioned under No. 150. Wrecked some buildings damaged by the preceding. 152 1893 III 9 0 35 VI Central Luzon. Very strong earthquake in the Provinces of Nueva Vizcaya, Benguet, and Pangasinan. 153 1893 IV 12 13 48 VI Very strong earthquake in Camarines, Albay, Sorsogon, Masbate, and northern Samar. Its epicenter was close to Masbate Island. 154 1893 VI 3 6 23 VII Violent earthquake in the whole western part of Mindanao, proceeding from the neighborhood of Illana Bay. No. Date. Intensity. Epicenter and effects. *Y. M. d. h. m.* 155 1893 VI 21 14 50 X Disastrous earthquake in the Agusan River Valley. The fact that there was no general destruction of buildings with heavy loss of life is due solely to the circumstance that the region affected contained only structures of bamboo and nipa. The effects of the convulsions on the topography of the region give an idea of what the consequences of the quake might have been had it found another class of buildings. There are indications that in the southern part of the valley an area of many square kilometers subsided to a considerable extent. Repetitions were frequent throughout an entire year. 156 1893 VII 1 4 8 VII Very violent earthquake in the valley of the Agusan River. 157 1893 XII 24 0 24 VI Very strong earthquake in southeastern Luzon, northern Samar, and Masbate. The epicenter lay northeast of Masbate Island, close to Capul Island, on which latter the quake was violent. Repeated at 18h 2m of the same day. 158 1894 II 10 0 42 VIII Destructive earthquake in southeastern Mindanao, having its epicenter in the region east of Davao Gulf. It produced many fissures and displacements in the mountains and cracked a few houses of wood in the towns of Mati and Sigaboy. The aftershocks continued on the 10th and 11th, occurring at intervals of about 5 minutes. 159 1894 II 18 5 23 VI Very strong earthquake in the valley of the Agusan River which was repeated with the same intensity at 23h 58m of the 19th. 160 1894 IV 2 2 34 VI Very strong earthquake in central Luzon, especially in Nueva Ecija, Pangasinan, and Benguet. 161 1894 VI 29 2 57 VIII Agusan

River Valley. Destructive earthquake whose effects were similar to those of the earthquake on June 21, 1893 (No. 155). The aftershocks, which had been felt ever since the latter disturbance, increased in force and frequency. 162 1894 VI 30 5 50 VII Violent earthquake in Agusan River Valley. Repeated with the same intensity at 20h 8m. 163 1895 V 14 6 42 VII Northern Mindoro. Very violent earthquake which damaged considerably the church and *convento* at Calapan, these being the only masonry buildings in the town. It was repeated with great intensity at 23h 52m of the same day and at 0h 3m of the 17th. On the 14th more than 40 aftershocks of variable intensity were counted. 164 1895 VI 7 21 56 VII Northern Mindoro. Very violent earthquake which ruined part of the church at Calapan. Severe repetitions occurred at 4h 0m and 6h 26m of the 8th. 165 1896 IX 13 12 58 VII Northwestern Luzon. Very violent earthquake which damaged several buildings in Laoag and other towns of Ilocos Norte. Strong repetitions at 16h 45m and 17h 10m. 166 1897 I 18 2 35 VI Very strong earthquake in the Mountain Province and the Provinces of Isabela and Cagayan. Numerous aftershocks followed during the day. 167 1897 II 16 5 4 VII Agusan River Valley. Violent earthquake with daily aftershocks during the rest of the month. No. Date. Intensity. Epicenter and effects. *Y. M. d. h. m.* 168 1897 IV 8 21 20 VIII Agusan River Valley. Destructive earthquake. 169 1897 V 13 19 22 VIII Masbate Island. Destructive earthquake which heavily damaged several buildings, bridges, and wharves. A strong repetition occurred at 14h 9m of the 15th. Weak aftershocks were frequent until the 27th. 170 1897 VIII 15 20 17 VIII Ilocos Sur. Destructive earthquake with epicentric area of 50 kilometers in length and 20 kilometers in width. The towns which suffered most were those between Candon and Vigan. 171 1897 IX 21 3 10 VII Very violent earthquake in northwestern Mindanao. It produced fissures in the ground and slightly injured buildings in the district of Dapitan. More than 36 aftershocks of varying intensity were recorded during the next 10 hours. 172 1897 IX 21 13 15 IX Disastrous earthquake in the district of Zamboanga, Basilan, and Jolo Islands. It wrought great destruction of buildings and produced fissures, landslides, and similar effects. A formidable "tsunami" (tidal wave) claimed hundreds of victims on the western shores of Basilan. This "tsunami" was the most imposing recorded in the seismological history of the Archipelago. There followed innumerable

26

aftershocks during 18 months, 200 having been counted before the middle of October, of which those on September 22, 23, 24, 26, and 29, and October 12 and 15 deserve special mention on account of their great intensity. 173 1897 X 8 5 0 VI Very strong earthquake in the district of Davao. 174 1897 X 19 8 5 IX Northern Samar. Destructive earthquake which damaged to a considerable extent buildings in Sulat, Palapag, Catubic, Oras, Gandara, and Laoang, towns near the northern and northeastern coasts of the island, and also produced vast fissures and other notable effects which resulted in the destruction of various bridges and roads. 175 1897 X 19 15 15 VIII Northern Samar. Most violent earthquake, with results similar to those of the preceding, though less severe. Countless aftershocks continued until the following April, those of October 19, 20, and 21 being the strongest. 176 1897 XI 14 8 59 VII Very violent earthquake, but of very limited epicentral area, in Ilocos Sur, northwestern Luzon. It wrecked the church at Candon. 177 1898 I 30 19 15 VII Sulu Archipelago. Violent earthquake, preceded by two of less severity at 18h 10m and 18h 36m. 178 1899 XII 26 4 20 VI Very strong earthquake in the Agusan River Valley. 179 1900 VIII 14 4 14 VI Very strong earthquake in Masbate and northern Cebu. 180 1901 IX 10 8 30 VII Very violent earthquake in eastern Tayabas; damaged the church of Calauag and other towns on the eastern shores of Lamon Bay. Large fissures opened on the beach and the water became very turbid; dead fishes were likewise found. 181 1901 XII 15 6 58 VII Very violent earthquake in southern Luzon. Some towns in Batangas Province suffered slight damage. No. Date. Intensity. Epicenter and effects. *Y. M. d. h. m.* 182 1902 VII 12 21 47 VI Northeastern Mindanao. Very strong earthquake with epicenter in Butuan Bay. Two repetitions, which occurred on the 13th, showed little intensity. 183 1902 VIII 21 19 17 X Southwestern Mindanao. Destructive earthquake in the Lanao and Cotabato districts. It proceeded from the center which lies in the northern part of Illana Bay, and caused heavy damage to all the buildings in the towns and in the Moro villages and strongholds within the meizoseismal region. The effects were extraordinary on land as well as within the bay; in the latter the telegraph cables were found broken and buried by débris. It is assumed as certain that there were many lives lost in the Moro forts, but their number is not known. The aftershocks were so frequent that some 400 could be counted within the first 8 days after the disaster, some 10 or 12 of these reaching force VI and VII. 184 1902 VIII 26 1 9 IX Province of Iloilo, Panay. Destructive earthquake which seriously damaged the churches and other buildings in the towns of Maasin, Calinog, and Janiuay. Many fissures opened in the mountains and extensive subsidences took place. The disturbance was preceded by an extraordinary noise, which was audible at great distances from the epicentral region. The reports do not mention a single aftershock. 185 1902 XI 17 8 38 VII Southwestern Luzon. Very violent earthquake in the Provinces of Batangas, Cavite, Bataan and Zambales. The effects were confined to slight damages to several buildings in Batangas, Taal, and other towns south and west of Taal Volcano. The epicenter was near the coasts of southwestern Luzon, where intense subterranean noises were heard. The 7 aftershocks which have been recorded were of little intensity. 186 1903 V 24 6 11 VI Southeastern Mindanao. Very intense earthquake, having its center to the northwest of Davao Gulf. The shock was perceptible throughout the island. 187 1903 XII 28 10 56 VIII Destructive earthquake in the region east of Davao Gulf which damaged many houses in Mati, Caraga, Sigaboy, etc. Large fissures opened and several displacements occurred in the limestone layers of the Pacific coast near Caraga. A few aftershocks were felt on the 29th and 30th. 188 1904 X 1 18 16 VII Very violent earthquake in the southern part of the Agusan River Valley. 189 1904 X 9 2 39 VII Northern Luzon. Very violent earthquake whose epicenter lay in the northern part of the Mountain Province. Slight damage was done in several towns of Ilocos Norte and Cagayan, situated near the Central Cordillera. 190 1905 XII 8 16 22 VII Very violent earthquake in southeastern Luzon and the eastern Visayas. Its epicenter lay underneath the sea, to the south of Masbate Island. No. Date. Intensity. Epicenter and effects. *Y. M. d. h. m.* 191 1905 XII 11 2 12 VIII Agusan River Valley. Destructive earthquake, which left its history written on the topography of the region, but made little impression upon the buildings, as these were of bamboo and palm leaves. The shock was well felt throughout Mindanao and the eastern Visayas. 192 1906 VI 19 19 23 VI Batanes Islands. Violent earthquake accompanied by subterranean noises. It proceeded from a center situated south of Balintang Channel, and showed likewise considerable intensity in northern Luzon. The 20th and 21st witnessed many aftershocks. 193 1907 IV 19 5 0 IX Camarines Province. Destructive earthquake which, within an area of 200 kilometers in length and

60 in width, wrecked many masonry buildings, produced great fissures in the ground and landslides in the mountains. Only two cases of death and a few of injuries received have been recorded. 194 1907 IV 19 7 53 VII Very violent earthquake in the same region as the preceding. It completed the ruin of some buildings weakened by its predecessor. These two earthquakes were followed by numerous aftershocks of varying intensity until the month of July. 195 1907 V 20 15 49 VIII Southern Leyte. Very violent earthquake with a very intense repetition at 16h 3m. The meizoseismic area had a diameter of only 10 kilometers, determined by an extinct volcano, Mount Cabalían, which is situated in this part of the island. From May 17 to 25 some 60 earthquakes of various intensities were felt. No enhanced activity was observed in the volcano, but many fissures and great landslides were produced on its slopes. 196 1907 V 25 23 52 VIII Northern Luzon. Very violent earthquake whose center was in the northern part of the Central Cordillera (Mountain Province). It did considerable damage in the Provinces of Ilocos Norte and Cagayan. The central part of the epicentral region, where the effects must have been more severe, is inhabited exclusively by wild tribes. No aftershocks have been recorded. 197 1907 XI 24 21 59 IX Camarines Province. Destructive earthquake which ruined nearly all the masonry buildings of the towns within an area of some 30 kilometers in length and 20 in width. Within this small region, composed of recent alluvial soil and traversed by the Quinali River, a great number of fissures opened and various subsidences took place. 198 1908 I 21 4 5 VI Western Leyte. Very strong earthquake proceeding from a submarine center not far from Ormoc Bay. It was followed by two very intense aftershocks at 4h 30m and 7h 57m and many of less severity until the 23d. 199 1908 III 5 10 20 VI Agusan River Valley. Very strong earthquake. 200 1908 V 14 21 18 VI Very strong earthquake in western Mindanao and the Sulu Archipelago. No. Date. Intensity. Epicenter and effects. *Y. M. d. h. m.* 201 1909 II 7 0 1 VI Very strong earthquake in the region south of Butuan Bay. Its epicentral area was very small, comprising only Butuan and the towns close to the mouth of the Agusan River. 202 1909 III 18 16 30 VIII Eastern Mindanao. Very violent earthquake whose epicenter stretched in a narrow belt along parallel 8° 12' latitude north from the Agusan River to the Pacific coast. It did severe damage to the church and *convento* of Bislig and in some neighboring towns. 203 1909 IV 14

6 37 VI Very strong earthquake in the extreme southeast of Luzon, having its center underneath the sea to the south of Catanduanes Island.

APPENDIX.

EARTHQUAKES IN THE MARIANAS ISLANDS.

No. Date. Intensity. Epicenter and effects. *Y. M. d. h. m.* 1 1825 IV — — — VIII Destructive earthquake in the Marinas or Ladrones group of islands. Ruined many buildings at Agaña, Guam Island. 2 1834 V — — — VIII Destructive earthquake on Guam Island. Considerable havoc and great panic at Agaña and in the other towns of the island. 3 1849 I 25 14 56 IX Destructive earthquake. Laid in ruins all the masonry buildings on the islands—the church, *convento*, and college at Agaña, the churches at Umata, Pago, and Agat, together with a great number of houses. Immense fissures opened in many places, and an extraordinary commotion of short duration was observed in the sea. There followed countless aftershocks, some of them very intense; from January 25 to March 11 no fewer than 150 were actually counted. 4 1862 VII 1 7 48 VII Violent earthquake. Did great damage to the tile roofs at Agaña and in other towns on the Island of Guam. 5 1863 XII 7 3 — VI Guam. Violent earthquake causing great alarm but little harm. 6 1866 VI 24 13 — VI Guam. Very strong earthquake. 7 1870 V 13 15 27 VI Guam. Two very strong shocks at an interval of 10 seconds. The fact that they did no damage has been attributed to the absence of horizontal movements. 8 1892 V 16 21 10 VIII Destructive earthquake which severely damaged the masonry buildings in Agaña and other towns, produced many fissures and displacements on the coasts and in other places. The sea retired suddenly, but no devastating alternations of floods and ebbs followed. The few aftershocks which occurred during the two following days were feeble. 9 1902 IX 22 11 15 IX Destructive earthquake which wrecked or damaged very seriously all the buildings at Agaña, Guam. Great fissures opened in the ground and displacements occurred which resulted in the destruction of several bridges. Similar effects are reported from Saipan Island. Personal accidents were limited to a few injured. Aftershocks were very numerous during the first days after the earthquake. 10 1902 XII 24 7 15 VI Very strong earthquake lasting over a minute. At this time the aftershocks of the earthquake of September 22 were still continuing. 11 1903 II 10 12 39 VII Guam. Violent earthquake which damaged to some extent the government house at Agaña. Two distinct series of shocks were observed, having a total duration of more than a minute. No. Date. Intensity. Epicenter and effects. *Y. M. d. h. m.* 12 1909 XII 10 9 0 VIII Guam. Destructive earthquake. Two shocks lasting 20 seconds, of which the second was the more severe. Direction of the shocks SE-NW. In Agaña practically all the east and west walls of native mortar houses were badly cracked. In nearly every house articles on shelves of these walls were thrown down, while those on the north and south sides remained in place. The women's hospital, built of local mortar, was so badly injured as to require tearing down; its tiled roof slid off to westward and the worst cracks were in the east wall. Many ceiling boards in different houses were shaken down. Several fissures opened in the ground, from one of which, near the river, came a large flow of water. The river bed sank in several places. The passing wave could be seen distinctly as it crossed the plaza, and the station ship in the harbor reported having felt the shock. No damage of importance was done in the other towns on the island. The buildings of the cable station at Sumay, constructed of reinforced concrete, were not injured, but a few objects were thrown down and the steel water towers could be seen swaying. No shocks were noticed before or after the earthquake, nor was anything extraordinary observed in the sea. The disturbance was not felt at Yap, Western Carolines. No information from the other islands.

Map of the Philippine Islands
        Click on map for larger image.

Earthquake Map of the Philippine Islands 1599-1909
    Click on map for larger image.

    Typographical errors corrected in text:

Page 10:   neihgboring replaced with neighboring
Page 10:   Iloílo replaced with Iloilo
Page 11:   Iloílo replaced with Iloilo
Page 21:   damage replaced with damaged

www.ingramcontent.com/pod-product-compliance
Lightning Source LLC
Chambersburg PA
CBHW071320280526

45788CB00004B/1966